HARD QUESTIONS

HARD QUESTIONS

THE SERIAL INTELLECTUAL

Innovative Industries 1, LLC

CONTENTS

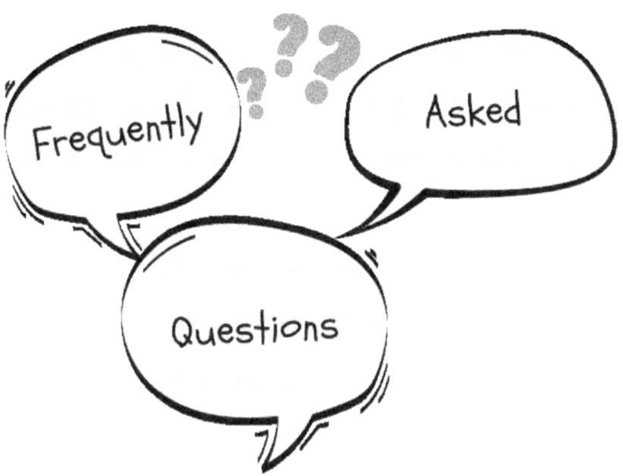
Frequently
Asked
Questions

CHAPTER 1

FAQs ABOUT QUESTIONS

Questions are a fundamental tool for human communication, learning, and problem-solving. They serve various purposes, including seeking information, encouraging critical thinking, eliciting opinions, and facilitating discussion. Questions also help clarify doubts, stimulate curiosity, and guide exploration.

Questions are used in various contexts, such as education, research, interviews, surveys, therapy, and everyday conversations. They can be open-ended (e.g., "What are your thoughts on this?") or closed-ended (e.g., "Is it raining?"). How questions are framed and asked depends on the desired outcome and the context.

The use of questions as a method of inquiry can be traced back to ancient civilizations. In particular, the ancient Greeks, with philosophers like Socrates, played a pivotal role in shaping the concept of the "Socratic method." Socrates believed in the power of asking questions to stimulate critical thinking and encourage individuals to examine their beliefs and knowledge.

Socrates, who lived in Athens in the fifth century BCE, is often credited with formalizing the Socratic method, a dialectical approach to philosophical discussions. He would converse with fellow citizens, posing open-ended questions designed to challenge assumptions and prompt deeper thought. This method is still influential in modern pedagogy and critical thinking. In the medieval period, particularly during the scholastic tradition of the twelfth to seventeenth centuries, scholars like Thomas Aquinas used questions extensively in their writings. The scholastics employed a systematic approach to questions, dissecting complex theological and philosophical issues into questions and answers.

During the Renaissance and Enlightenment eras, the use of questions in intellectual discourse continued to evolve. Thinkers like René Descartes employed the method of doubt and posed foundational questions, such as *Cogito, ergo sum* ("I think, therefore I am"). This period also saw the rise of empirical questions in the natural sciences. Various authors have used questions to create engaging narratives. In Shakespeare's plays, for instance, characters often pose existential and moral questions, contributing to the exploration of complex themes. In the twentieth century, the field of psychology started to delve into the psychology of questions. Educational psychologists like Benjamin Bloom emphasized the role of questioning in promoting higher-order thinking skills and cognitive development. Educational systems worldwide incorporate questions as a fundamental part of teaching and assessment.

Questions are critical to research methodologies in social sciences and other disciplines. Researchers use questions to frame their inquiries, design surveys, and collect data. The development of questionnaires and interviews as research tools is a testament to the importance of questions in academic investigations. The digital age has seen the rise of search engines and question-answering platforms that have transformed how people seek information.

Throughout history, individuals have risen to prominence and left an indelible mark on the world. These significant figures, be they political leaders, scientists, philosophers, or artists, have often been defined by the questions they posed, the challenges they undertook, and the ideas they pursued. Socrates asked the fundamental question, "Know thyself." He believed that true wisdom comes from understanding one's limitations and biases. Socratic inquiry laid the foundation for Western philosophy and the pursuit of self-awareness, challenging individuals to examine their beliefs, values, and actions. Galileo Galilei, the Italian scientist, revolutionized our understanding of the cosmos by asking "What does the night sky reveal?" His telescopic observations of the stars and planets challenged the prevailing geocentric view of the universe and set the stage for the scientific method and the Copernican Revolution.

"What is the nature of reality?" The question of reality's nature has been at the heart of philosophical and scientific inquiry for centuries. From the ancient Greeks pondering the elements to the quantum physicists of the twentieth century, this question has spurred countless discoveries and paradigm shifts. The answers to this question have fundamentally altered our understanding of the universe and led to innovations ranging from electricity to the internet.

"How can we achieve social justice?" The quest for social justice is a question that has driven movements for equality and human rights throughout history. The abolition of slavery, the suffrage of women, and the fight against racial discrimination all emerged from a fundamental question about fairness and equality. It's a question that continues to reshape our societies, leading to legal reforms, social movements, and changes in how we view one another.

"What is the meaning of life?" This existential question has occupied the minds of philosophers, theologians, and thinkers across cultures and centuries. It has inspired art, literature, and religious beliefs, leading to the formation of ethical systems and ideologies. The pursuit of meaning has shaped individual lives and influenced the collective values of societies.

"How can we harness the power of technology?" As humans, we are driven by curiosity and the question of using technology to enhance our lives. The question has propelled us to innovate and create, from the invention of the printing press to the development of artificial intelligence. Technology has changed the world and will continue to do so as we explore our inventions' ethical and practical implications.

"What is the role of government?" The question of governance and its purpose has shaped the world's political landscape. From the ancient civilizations of Mesopotamia to modern democratic societies, this question has led to revolutions, the drafting of constitutions, and the establishment of legal systems. It influences how we organize and structure our societies, addressing issues such as power, representation, and social welfare.

These questions, among others, have been instrumental in driving change and progress throughout history. They have challenged our thinking, motivated exploration, and ignited the fires of creativity and innovation. The answers may evolve over time, but the questions themselves will continue to play a crucial role in shaping the world we live in and the world we aim to create.

Common Places Where Questions Are Found

In philosophy, questions are the primary tool for engaging in deep, critical thinking. Philosophers ponder fundamental questions about existence, ethics, and knowledge. Scientific inquiry revolves around asking questions. Scientists formulate hypotheses and design experiments to find answers, pushing the boundaries of human knowledge. In healthcare, questions guide diagnostic processes and treatment decisions. Physicians ask questions to understand patients' symptoms and medical histories.

The field of education centers on asking questions to foster learning. Educators use queries to engage students, prompt discussions, and assess understanding. Legal professionals employ questions to gather evidence, examine witnesses, and cross-examine in court, helping to determine the truth. Historians ask questions about the past, exploring the causes and consequences of historical events and uncovering forgotten stories. Psychologists use questions to delve into the human mind and behavior, from inquiries about emotions and cognition to mental health assessments. In the corporate world, questions drive market research, customer feedback, and strategic decision-making to understand consumer preferences. Journalists seek answers to the "five W's and one H" (who, what, where, when, why, and how) to provide accurate and informative news stories.

Astronomers explore the universe by posing questions about the cosmos, its origins, and the nature of celestial bodies. Environmental scientists ask questions about ecosystems, climate change, and sustainability to address pressing environmental challenges. Engineers pose questions to solve practical problems, from designing bridges and buildings to creating new technologies. Artists and creative professionals use questions as a source of inspiration and to provoke thought about the meaning and impact of their work. Spiritual leaders and theologians explore profound questions about the divine, faith, and the meaning of life.

Coaches and athletes ask questions about strategy, training methods, and performance improvement. Musicians ask questions about melody, harmony, and rhythm to compose songs and orchestrate complex musical pieces. Architects use questions to shape their designs, considering functionality, aesthetics, and sustainability. Geologists inquire about the Earth's structure, geological processes, and natural resources, seeking answers hidden beneath the Earth's surface. Chefs and food enthusiasts ask questions about ingredients, techniques, and flavors to create innovative and delicious dishes. In the realm of technology, questions fuel innovation by challenging the status quo and exploring possibilities for future developments.

The Bible contains numerous questions; the exact count can vary depending on the translation. Some Bibles may contain over three thousand questions. These questions cover many topics, from theological and moral inquiries to practical and historical ones.

The Quran contains various questions, but an exact count can be challenging due to differences in translations and interpretations. Such questions are used to prompt reflection, instruct, and emphasize key theological concepts. Some sources estimate there are over three hundred questions in the Quran.

Jewish texts, including the Torah and Talmud, contain many questions. These questions serve to explore religious and ethical matters, legal interpretations, and discussions of moral and philosophical dilemmas. An exact count would be difficult to ascertain as it varies depending on the specific text and interpretation.

Dictionary
Hard Questions
Edition

HARD QUESTIONS DEFINED AND ILLUSTRATED

In the realm of problem-solving and intellectual inquiry, not all questions are created equal. Some questions are straightforward, with readily available answers, while others present a significant challenge, demanding rigorous thought, creative problem-solving, and sometimes even a multidisciplinary approach. These demanding questions are often referred to as "Hard Questions," and they serve as the crucible in which our intellectual growth and innovation are forged.

A hard question is a question that challenges a person's or entity's history, paradigms, beliefs and behaviors, and makes them uncomfortable. Hard questions are characterized by their complexity, ambiguity, and the absence of a simple or readily available solution. These questions require a deeper understanding of the problem, a combination of various skills and knowledge domains, and, often, significant research or experimentation to arrive at a satisfactory answer.

Consider the famous Traveling Salesman Problem (TSP). The challenge is to find the shortest route that visits a given set of cities and returns to the starting town. Although it might sound like a simple task for a handful of cities, as the number of cities increases, solving this problem becomes increasingly challenging. TSP is an example of a hard question in optimization and computational complexity.

In this case, a hard question emerges from the desire to optimize a real-world scenario. However, hard questions can be found in various domains, from mathematics and science to philosophy and social sciences.

Hard questions resist easy answers, requiring us to explore multiple facets and consider various perspectives, often leading us to reflect on our values, beliefs, and assumptions. These inquiries delve into the core of human existence, ethics, and the mysteries of the universe. They push the boundaries of our knowledge and understanding, prompting us to seek out new insights and engage in profound discussions.

To better understand what makes a question "hard," let's explore some of its defining characteristics:

Hard questions often lack clarity or present multiple interpretations. Solving them requires disentangling complex and intertwined factors. Questions about the nature of consciousness fall into this category. What is consciousness, and how does it arise in the human brain? These questions are difficult to answer due to the ambiguity of consciousness itself. Hard questions frequently cross the boundaries of traditional disciplines, demanding insights from diverse fields; solving them requires a collaborative, interdisciplinary approach. Addressing climate change involves science, policy, economics, and social aspects. Solving this global challenge necessitates cooperation among experts in various fields, reflecting the multidisciplinary nature of many hard questions.

Hard questions may be underpinned by inherent uncertainty or limited data, making it difficult to arrive at a definitive answer. Predicting stock market movements is challenging due to the multitude of factors influencing markets and the inherent unpredictability of human behavior.

These questions often involve intricate systems, intricate structures, and multifaceted processes. As a result, they are challenging to analyze and solve.

Hard Questions can evolve as knowledge advances and our understanding deepens. What was once considered an unsolvable problem may become tractable with new insights or technology.

Examples of hard questions abound daily, touching upon various aspects of our existence. One common category of hard questions revolves around morality and ethics. Questions like "Is it ever justified to lie?" or "What is the ethical approach to distributing limited medical resources during a pandemic?" challenge us to consider the balance between honesty, compassion, and fairness.

Existential questions often occupy our thoughts, making us ponder the purpose of our existence. "What is the meaning of life?" and "What happens after we die?" are hard questions that have perplexed philosophers, theologians, and individuals from all walks of life for centuries. These inquiries force us to confront the unknown and wrestle with our mortality.

In essence, hard questions are the crucible of intellectual growth and innovation. They push us to expand our horizons, encourage cross-disciplinary collaboration, and stimulate the development of new methods and tools to find answers.

Hard questions serve as catalysts for progress. They stimulate critical thinking, foster creativity, and drive innovation. They challenge our existing knowledge and spur us to explore uncharted territories, propelling humanity forward.

Case File #2024
Hard Questions, The Serial Intellectual

CHAPTER 3

A CASE FOR HARD QUESTIONS

I will present an argument in favor of hard questions, emphasizing their utility, value, and relevance in our personal, family, organizational, business, and institutional realms. To do so, I must build a case for three primary reasons.

First, humans are not naturally inclined toward challenging endeavors. The world continually offers easier alternatives for completing tasks, removing complexity from them. Humans are inherently averse to pain, and our bodies instinctively recoil from it. Consequently, when the term "hard questions" is mentioned, our natural response is to move away from them rather than toward them. Therefore, explaining why we should approach hard questions becomes necessary.

Second, historically, hard questions have not been viewed favorably. This perception may stem from their misuse by abusive individuals or from our earliest recollections, influenced by movies, TV shows, or family histories, which have shaped and tainted our perspectives on the hard remainder of this chapter; I will endeavor to persuade you of this belief. Hard questions should find their place in our lives, families, businesses, organizations, and institutions. What I mean by "having a home" is that they should hold a regular position. What I mean by "regular" is that they should be used frequently, so much so that we don't keep track of their use because they are a normal part of our lives. Nevertheless, the fact remains that hard questions, like many aspects of life, possess significant potential for positive application. A case requires presentation, given the prevalent perception that hard questions are not inherently beneficial.

Thirdly, I firmly believe in the immense utility of hard questions. They should become a customary aspect of our lives. In an average home, one encounters everyday items such as pots, pans, utensils, toilet paper, and various other household necessities.

These items are found in a home because people reside in homes and derive regular benefits from using them. This analogy illustrates my point; hard questions should occupy a place in our lives, families, businesses, organizations, and institutions. Hard questions constitute the most valuable and effective tools for fostering relationships. To the best of my knowledge, nothing surpasses their effectiveness. Hard questions are our most valuable asset. It's important to recognize their worth, much like we view gold. And how do we treat gold? We secure it, placing it in a safe location to protect it from theft and ensure its preservation, as its value is intrinsic. Hard questions are unparalleled in their capacity to generate, nurture, maintain, and enhance our personal development, holistic family well-being, organizational and business worth, and institutional effectiveness.

Hard questions possess unmatched capabilities in revelation and discovery, akin to MRI, CAT scans, X-rays, and blood tests. When utilized appropriately, they can substantially aid us in our quest for personal and organizational well-being and prosperity. Their effectiveness lies in their capacity to challenge our history, paradigms, beliefs, behaviors, and methodologies. Hard questions induce discomfort. Discomfort is the most transformative experience known to humanity. Comfort rarely brings about change, while discomfort has been instrumental in transforming countless individuals. Everything in life that holds value comes with a price tag. The price tag on hard questions involves momentary discomfort, but the reward reaped from addressing them is the transformative change we yearn for.

CHAPTER 4

HARD QUESTIONS IN REDEMPTIVE HISTORY

One of the integral components of redemptive history is hard questions. The definition of redemptive history is the Bible's account of the commencement of history, the events that unfolded within it, the actions of God, the ongoing actions of God, and the impending conclusion of it all. Many of you know I follow the Christian faith, and my study of the Bible spans over three decades. However, in all of these years, I have never seen the abundance of the hard questions in the Bible. During the pandemic and shortly after, I assumed a leadership role where I was forced to engage with and answer hard questions about my role and the organization I was leading. Simultaneously, as I was reading the Bible, I noticed how many hard questions were in it. This discovery led to a new perspective on the Bible. It took me back to the beginning of the Bible, specifically the initial chapters of Genesis, in search of hard questions. Realizing the prominent role questions played within the Bible was somewhat surprising. Upon reaching Genesis chapter three, the serpent's interaction with Adam and Eve involved a question. Subsequently, as I continued to explore the Bible, I saw that it is full of questions. Questions from God, questions posed by individuals in their relationship with God, and challenging questions were encountered in nearly every genre of the scripture.

I concluded that questions are not foreign aspects of religion but rather an inherent component. It is common practice for God's people to ask God questions and for God to respond with questions. The Bible presents a variety of questions, some with profound depth, while others can be quite painful. Specific questions are revelatory, revealing the most intimate aspects of our hearts and minds, while others are humorous. One aspect remains unmistakable: not only does God use questions, but so do other individuals in the Bible. Furthermore, these questions, far from being merely employed, are regarded as strategic tools in the hands of the authors of the Bible. The question is what significance does all this hold for you, the reader, and for me, the writer?

This idea signifies the close connection between religion and hard questions. The notion that faith eliminates questions does not find its origins in the Bible. The belief that religious establishments should be exempt from hard questions cannot be deduced from the sacred texts they profess to adopt. In reality, it's quite the contrary. No individual, entity, organization, or life situation exists where hard questions from God and others should be prohibited. It is a typical contemporary belief that one of life's objectives is to attain immunity from difficult questions. One place where you can see this phenomenon is in the arena of politics, and it has played out throughout American and global history.

Indeed, immunity from hard questions has been bestowed upon certain companies, organizations, and individuals. Nevertheless, the undeniable truth remains that a profound connection exists between religion and hard questions. It would be beneficial for all of us to grasp this connection and devise methods within our religious lives to pose hard questions to others, to our religious institutions, and occasionally even God. Simultaneously, we exhibit humility to accept and endeavor to respond to the hard questions posed by God, both past and future.

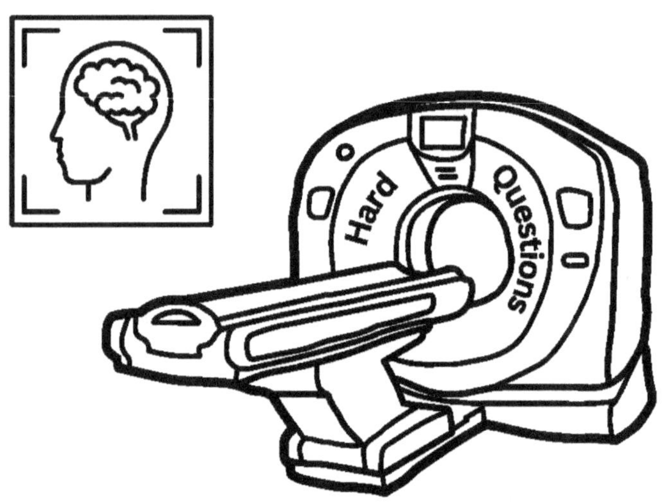

Hard
Questions

CHAPTER 5

USES OF HARD QUESTIONS

In this chapter, I would like to discuss some ways we can use hard questions, but before doing so, I want to address the elephant in the room. Like many things, we can use hard questions for good or evil. An evil person will use hard questions as weapons rather than allies. However, this shouldn't stop individuals, organizations, businesses, or any collective from using them for good.

First and foremost, their primary and most beneficial utilization is for *revelatory purposes.* Hard questions share similarities with medical diagnostic tools such as MRI, CAT scans, X-rays, blood tests, and scopes. Mentioning these tools may induce some anxiety, but their purpose is well-known. They provide doctors with information for improved assessment and treatment to either maintain or enhance our health. Hard questions operate similarly. They possess a revelatory nature; when used correctly, wisely, gently, yet resolutely, they can accomplish what an MRI achieves in an individual.

Furthermore, they can achieve similar results in a family, an organization, or any institution or entity. Hard questions' primary advantage lies in their ability to unveil information about a person or a thing. Due to this, all of us must employ them regularly, in every circumstance, using wise and compassionate approaches.

Additionally, a second function of hard questions is for ***confrontational purposes***. Regrettably, we live in a practical world where confronting reality is sometimes necessary. Certain issues persist and demand solutions and attention. Hard questions can serve as an effective means to achieve this.

A third function of hard questions is to ***gather information***. As previously mentioned, their revelatory aspect is something we encounter regularly. When consulting with medical professionals, they typically pose two, three, four, or sometimes more hard questions about our mental, physical, and emotional well-being to gather the information they need to prescribe the proper treatment.

Fourth, some individuals use hard questions to ***test people***. We see this in law enforcement and in courtrooms, where lawyers are trained to use difficult questions to invoke responses or place people into particular predicaments.

Fifth, hard questions can be used ***rhetorically***. This employment entails posing questions with self-evident answers.

Emotion
Physiology
Culture
Past
Psychology
Spirituality
Hard
Questions

CHAPTER 6

RELATIONSHIPS

For us to optimize our use of hard questions, we must recognize and understand their relationship with six things.

The Relationships Between Emotions and Hard Questions

First, human emotions encompass a wide spectrum, but I would like to focus our attention on the emotional triumvirate: shame, fear, and guilt. Let's take a moment to contemplate the relationship between hard questions and these three emotions, beginning with shame. Shame is the feeling that something is wrong within oneself. It's an identity-based emotion. It is shame that instigates the desire to cover up.

Usually, shame fixates on the concept of one's image and how others perceive them. As a result, in a negative situation, hard questions tend to provoke sentiments of shame. Furthermore, shame frequently attempts to create preventative techniques to avoid answering hard questions. Hard questions are related to the primary fear of shame because they can unveil one's insufficiencies, exposing their inadequacy and broken-ness. Consequently, shame adopts various concealment methods, particularly through serving, achieving success, and cultivating a sense of distinctiveness. By excelling in these areas, individuals often avoid being asked hard questions.

Hard questions also share a relationship with fear. Fear is a proximity-based emotion obsessed with where one is and the safety associated with one's surroundings. Since fear is preoccupied with one's place and safety, it perceives hard questions as potential threats. To safeguard us, fear helps us identify sanctuaries. These sanctuaries may include our professional endeavors, productivity, presentation, or image. The necessity to conceal arises from the imperative need to avoid hard questions. Fear, when heightened to its extreme, takes on a phobic character, generating a mindset that, if left uncontrolled, can induce significant distress. Consequently, the connection between fear and hard questions is tangible for many individuals, often evoking intense, visceral responses to hard questions.

Hard questions also have a relationship with guilt. Guilt is a performance-based emotion we experience when we have engaged in something we should not have or neglected something we should have done. It's a reactionary emotion. Guilt doesn't typically like hard questions because its most significant concern is with the potential revelation of wrongful actions or the omission of necessary actions. In either scenario, this would contribute to the notion that we do not possess qualities of moral virtue, competence in our professional endeavors, effective parenting skills, or adherence to religious principles. Regardless of the subject matter, this emotion does not typically run toward hard questions.

The interconnection between hard questions and our emotional state is evident. The crucial aspect is cultivating self-awareness regarding the relationship between our emotions and hard questions. It's essential to recognize that our feelings typically seek to safeguard us, even when they become exaggerated, although their safeguarding intentions often result in harm. As I've emphasized in many of my other books, engaging with our emotions is the path to navigating this issue, progressing through it, and moving forward. This action involves comprehending them fully and ensuring that they operate in our favor rather than in opposition. This idea is particularly significant in the context of hard questions since we have already established that hard questions are beneficial for us. If our emotions deter us from them, they effectively hinder us from one of the most valuable tools at our disposal.

The Relationships Between Psychology and Hard Questions

Hard questions connect with our psychology, which, for practical purposes, is defined as how we perceive, process, and present ourselves to the world. Hard questions are subject to our perception. Each of us possess a distinct perspective of the world. Some consider it as a place where connections can be made, while others see it through the lens of conflict or adversity. Some seek secure havens within it. Our worldviews and perceptions of the world differ, but most people tend to gravitate toward one way in which they perceive it.

The main issue is not how people perceive the world but how aware they are of their perceptions. People tend to perceive hard questions as opportunities or threats, depending on their psychology and emotions. Their perceptions are why hard questions are often avoided in our lives, families, and organizations. Our psychology, together with our emotions, will govern how we approach and perceive complex topics. This truth is one of the key reasons we don't ask hard questions in our lives, families, or organizations—because many people regard them as potential threats, insults, and sources of strife and ruin. As a result, they try everything possible to avoid them.

We all have a way to perceive hard questions, but we also have a way to process them. Emotions serve as a method for some to process hard questions, which can pose challenges or offer incredible insights. The outcome is contingent on one's awareness and processing skills. Some individuals opt for a more analytical approach, using additional questions and more intricate questions. They are inherently analytical and require more information. In contrast, others process hard questions instinctually.

The path you take to discover your general processing tendencies allows you to apply that insight to your approach when tackling hard questions. I cannot emphasize the significance of this enough. It greatly aids in maximizing the utility of hard questions. Whether you function as a leader, manager, organizer, parent or within any other role involving relationships, you use hard questions. In that case, the insights discussed here will be exceptionally valuable.

We've discussed how perception and processing impact our relationship with hard questions. Now, let's examine the relationship between hard questions and how we present ourselves to the world. We all have an image of ourselves or a desired way we want to be viewed. Hard questions can pose a potential threat to the way we would like to present ourselves to others. This idea is especially true if we lack self-awareness. For example, if we present ourselves as relational, we could perceive a hard question as threat to our image. If we present ourselves as having it all figured out, hard questions might reveal that we don't have it all figured out. And if we present ourselves to the world as a person who is grounded, hard questions may reveal that we are standing on sand rather than a firm foundation. In all three illustrations, you can see that how we present ourselves can hinder us from benefitting from hard questions if we lack self-awareness.

To reiterate, being mindful of how we tend to present ourselves to the world and how we aspire to be perceived in it holds significant importance in our psychological relationship with hard questions.

The Relationship Between Physiology and Hard Questions

Discussing hard questions and their connection to emotions and psychology necessitates consideration of the interaction between our bodies and hard questions. Our bodies have a way in which they react to such questions. It is crucial to emphasize the importance of self-awareness regarding our bodily responses to hard questions. Hard questions are received orally through our ears, and various emotional reactions may arise, such as nervousness, anxiety, peace, or other feelings. Our bodies exhibit distinct responses when confronted with hard questions. Hard questions are often physiological triggers. Recognizing these triggers enables better preparation and enhanced readiness to receive and process hard questions, thus reaping the benefits we've discussed. Our bodies retain memories, so if past encounters with hard questions were challenging, your body would recall them. Consequently, when you face a situation involving hard questions, it should come as no surprise if your anxiety levels increase, or other reactions become apparent.

Because your body retains the previous experience with hard questions, its response aligns with your training, natural predisposition, or protective instincts. There should be no ambiguity about this: our bodies react to hard questions. The question is whether we know how our bodies store and handle hard questions. Additionally, physiology and its connection with hard questions, our bodies assume a specific posture. Some individuals lean in, while others lean out.

Some individuals adopt a posture that aligns with their emotional and psychological state as they enter into and engage with hard questions. Just as in the relationship between hard questions, emotions, and psychology, the crucial element is our awareness of how our bodies process hard questions.

The Relationship Between the Past and Hard Questions

During our discussion concerning the relationship hard questions share with our emotions, psychology, and physiology, we should not overlook the connection that hard questions hold with our past. Everyone who reads this book has encountered hard questions at some point in their personal history. Some individuals recollect their parents asking challenging questions and engaging in arguments and disputes. These questions could pertain to finances, substance abuse, or family issues. When we reflect upon our past experiences, many do not harbor pleasant memories regarding the role hard questions played during our youth. Unless we are conscious and endeavor to reposition it, the lasting effect is that it leaves a negative impression in our minds, bodies, and emotions concerning hard questions.

The argument here is straightforward: our past influences our perception of hard questions most. Therefore, if we intend to progress and harness the potential benefits of hard questions, it's highly probable that each of us will need to, at the very least, revisit our past and ensure that there are no lingering hindrances preventing us from embracing all the positive outcomes that hard questions can bring into our lives.

The Relationships Between Spirituality and Hard Questions

There is a notable connection with hard questions in the realm of spirituality. For this book section, spirituality is defined as one's relationship with God. In a previous chapter, I explained a little bit about my spiritual journey with hard questions that played a significant role in the writing of this book. This exploration revealed that hard questions are prevalent in the Bible. It became apparent that both God and God's people frequently pose questions.

Furthermore, questions are a significant teaching method employed by prophets, Jesus, apostles, and the Bible's writers. Thus, the conclusion is that questions are essential to one's spirituality. To expand upon this, asking questions is a fundamental characteristic of spirituality. This assertion is supported by the observation that we find God posing questions to us and people in the Bible asking questions of God.

Hence, the conclusion is that questions are normative, not the exception. They constitute a significant part of our spirituality. Furthermore, as mentioned in the earlier chapter, we must reject the notion that spirituality's purpose is to eradicate questions. I would propose that spirituality should elicit more questions. At some point in our lives, many of us have encountered the idea that a genuinely spiritual individual never questions God. My concern with this notion is that there are numerous individuals in the Bible and people I've known who were profoundly spiritual yet questioned God. The critical factor in questioning God is the motive and intent rather than the essence. Even in his final days, Jesus questioned God when he said "My God, why have you forsaken me?"

Our spirituality, particularly our growth, is to some extent reliant on our proficiency in handling, utilizing, and responding to the questions posed by God, ourselves, and others in our spiritual community. The more challenging these questions are, whether they originate from God, ourselves, or fellow travelers on the spiritual journey, the more genuine and comprehensive we can anticipate our spirituality becoming. In any instance where you encounter a wholesome and practical spirituality that aligns with what is found in the Bible, you will also observe a corresponding inclination towards engaging with hard questions within that individual.

The Relationship Between Culture and Hard Questions

The last area is the connection between hard questions and culture. Culture is intriguing because it encompasses both visible and concealed elements. It is both sensed and unfelt, evident yet discreet. Culture, along with all its components, language, behavior, beliefs, customs, paradigms, and structures, undoubtedly stands as the most influential force on the planet today. Consequently, it should not be surprising that hard questions maintain a relationship with culture. It is our culture that instructs us effectively or inadequately regarding hard questions. Our culture guides us in either avoiding or embracing hard questions. Our culture categorizes hard questions as negative or harmful or constructive or beneficial.

Our culture ultimately serves as the primary force in shaping how hard questions are perceived and processed—our culture endeavors to influence our feelings regarding hard questions. The prevalent approach to hard questions observed in most individuals within our culture tends to generate emotional pressure for us to conform. Indirectly and through habitual observation, our culture instructs us how to physically engage with hard questions or distance ourselves from them, defining our physical disposition toward them. This cultural instruction is predominantly unspoken and acquired through observation.

We must maintain complete awareness of our culture, comprehending its impact, attitudes, convictions, and conduct regarding hard questions. If we fail to do so, we will undoubtedly be shaped and swayed by it. Our culture mustn't obstruct our progress or deprive us of the advantages that hard questions can offer.

CHAPTER 7

WHERE DO HARD QUESTIONS LIVE?

Where do we find hard questions? There are places where you will see them and places where you will not see them. Why are they found in some places and not others? This chapter has two purposes: one, to help you understand the characteristics of the environments where hard questions are most likely to be found and two, to encourage individuals, families, organizations, businesses, or any other entity to embody these characteristics.

The first characteristic of an environment where we find hard questions is **safety**. Regarding safety, individuals should have confidence that no one intends to cause them harm. People need to believe that if they are asked a hard question, it will not result in any harm. Safety is not something that occurs without deliberate intention. To establish safety, one must consider all the safest places in our world today. They didn't simply emerge overnight. They were meticulously designed by an architect, an engineer, and a contractor, specifically focusing on safety. In our relationships and organizations, we often regard safety as an incidental outcome, assuming we can reside in it even when we haphazardly attempt to create it.

The second characteristic of an environment where we find hard questions is *vulnerability.* Not only should it be presented but also respected and protected. People will not willingly be vulnerable unless it is considered a valued trait. People will refrain from being vulnerable unless they perceive their vulnerability will be safeguarded. Thus, vulnerability must be respected and protected in organizations, businesses, families, or any context where hard questions are desired.

The third characteristic of an environment where we are likely to find hard questions is *trust.* When hard questions are raised, some will inevitably touch upon personal matters or have implications for individuals, businesses, budgets, or other sensitive areas. Without an environment that fosters trust and confidence, people will be disinclined to engage in hard questions. Practically speaking, the dialogue surrounding hard questions should be protected and held in confidentiality. Sometimes this means limiting the amount of people involved in the discussion and at times being very selective about who is involved in the process. And finally, there has to be consequences when trust is violated or people will not be inclined to ask and answer hard questions.

The fourth characteristic of an environment where we are sure to find hard questions is anywhere that prioritizes *personal development*. You will find hard questions thriving in an environment where everyone is committed to growth, improvement, and collaborative efforts to enhance effectiveness. When people are convinced that you support their betterment and are dedicated to pursuing a more fulfilling life, they are more likely to participate in hard questions.

The fifth characteristic of an environment where we find hard questions is one where asking hard questions is *exemplified.* One of the biggest problems I have seen is that we only use hard questions when things are at their worst. This tends to communicate all the wrong things about them. People need to see that hard questions are more than an emergency tool. They need to see that they are useful for everyday life. The best way for this to happen is if those in authority utilize them on a regular basis. People need to see others being asked hard things and then see them respond honestly, humbly, and openly. I really want to emphasize here that the initiative for making sure hard questions are being asked, answered and regularly used falls on whoever is in charge.

It is up to them to model this practice and to clearly communicate that being in authority does not exempt them from being subject to hard questions.

The sixth characteristic of an environment where we find hard questions is where people have ***secure identities.*** When hard questions are raised, individuals may feel unsettled, with their sense of self, role, belonging, likability, and acceptance called into question. Without a stable identity, they instinctively recoil from an environment with hard questions. Individuals in such situations will either attempt to cover information, seek refuge, and evade or embellish certain aspects to avoid confronting hard questions. Therefore it is very important for everyone who finds themselves in an environment where hard questions are being asked to have and cultivate an identity that is rooted and grounded in immovable and transcendent truths.

The seventh characteristic of an environment where you are likely to find hard questions is one that fosters ***mental and emotional well-being***. The path to holistic health has always involved the use of hard questions. Every person, family, organization and business that focuses on this type of health has used them and sees the value in them.

The eighth characteristic of an environment where we find hard questions is one where ***individuals are committed to repositioning their past*** to work for them and not against them. As previously discussed in the last chapter, a person's past experience with hard questions will shape how they perceive and process them. If these past experiences remain unaddressed, there will be a natural inclination to resist hard questions. Therefore, it is crucial in organizations, families, and any relational context for individuals to actively address and reposition their past to prevent it from becoming an obstacle.

The ninth characteristic of an environment where we find hard questions is one where they are seen as an asset.

Finally, the last characteristic of an environment where hard questions tend to exist is where people or organizations are ***self-aware.*** Hard questions mark the path to self-awareness. It's accurate to say that self-awareness is impossible without engaging with hard questions.

Therefore, one way to gauge an individual's, family's, organization's, or business' self-awareness is by assessing the prevalence of hard questions within them. Self-awareness involves desiring to understand yourself and how others perceive you in relationships. This definition applies universally, and anyone seeking positive outcomes seeks answers to these fundamental questions. Achieving these answers demands embarking on a journey through numerous hard questions.

OBSTACLES

Here are four of the biggest obstacles to hard questions:

One, *you and me*
Two, *them*
Three, *us* collectively
Four, any of the following social environments: *family, organizations, ethnicity, business, states, nations, or our world*

Hard + questions
= ?

HOW TO FORMULATE HARD QUESTIONS

This book is written to provide a resource for individuals, families, and leaders of organizations, institutions, and businesses. I frequently receive inquiries about how to craft hard questions. Therefore, I offer some practical recommendations on how to generate hard questions for yourself.

The first step in formulating hard questions involves identifying the questions that must be asked through an *assessment.* To do this, consider the following questions:

1. What is causing the most pain in the personal, family, organizational, business, or institutional context?
2. What have I or we heard people complain about the most?
3. What do you think we can do to solve these challenges?

The second step in formulating hard questions is to consider whether there is *anything currently posing a threat* to personal health or development and organizational, business, or institutional well-being. The reason for this is simple: when people perceive that they are in danger, they will be closed off to hard questions because the number one priority is to protect themselves. Another way to assess whether or not the threat is in the environment is to ask a question like this. Are there any aspects in our lives, organizations, businesses, or institutions that, if left unattended, could lead to significant issues within the next ninety days?

These questions will guide us in shaping the hard questions that require immediate attention. It's crucial to remember that when formulating hard questions, they should challenge our personal or collective history, paradigms, beliefs, and behaviors in a discomforting manner. It's worth noting that if a question fails to make you or the collective uncomfortable, it does not qualify as a hard question. Discomfort serves as a tool that propels us toward solutions and change. Now, you are ready to formulate and ask some hard questions.

Practical Suggestions

CHAPTER 10

PRACTICAL SUGGESTIONS FOR ASKING

Creating environments where hard questions can be posed is crucial, and an entire chapter has been dedicated to outlining the necessary characteristics for these settings to facilitate the exchange of hard questions and derive benefits from them. Here are six practical recommendations for posing hard questions and establishing a conducive environment.

First, ***schedule specific times for asking hard questions.*** Planning is essential, as unplanned endeavors often yield undesired outcomes. Regularly organize times to navigate through hard questions.

Second, before presenting hard questions, ***affirm the individuals or entities.*** Affirming individuals communicates that they are acknowledged, listened to, believed, and cared for. Before asking hard questions, allocating time for affirmations directed toward people and the concerned entity is imperative. This crucial second step is often overlooked and the results are rarely good. When we do this we resemble a doctor with poor bedside manners, rushing straight into the solutions with explaining the context and reasons why this solution is the best. By doing this we miss an opportunity to invest in people and to communicate how much we value them and or the entity we are working in.

Third, make sure you do a thorough and ***honest assessment*** before you start asking hard questions. This is going to help you in a number of ways. One, it's going to communicate that you care to know what's going on and value what people think. Two, it will help you to know which hard questions need to be asked. And three, it will help you implement them in the most effective way.

Fourth, it's important to provide ***assurance*** to people prior to asking them hard questions. People can be unsettled through the process and experience a lot of different emotions and thoughts and end up in worst case scenarios. One way to avoid that is by giving them assurances up front. Be honest with them about the process. The more they know the less they will tend to worry. Let them know that its normal to feel a little discomfort and uneasiness. Assure them that the goal is not hurt them but to solve the challenges you/they are facing. Let them know that they are not alone and that this is going to be a joint venture.

Fifth, here are some tips for you to consider when you are ***asking hard questions.*** When asking questions, creating space for all in the room to respond is crucial. In cases where the group is sizable or time is limited, allocating specific time slots for each person's response ensures that everyone has an opportunity to contribute. Recognizing that certain individuals may be reserved and prefer not to verbalize their thoughts, acknowledging their contribution through their physical presence is essential. Additionally, acknowledging that some individuals may prefer to express themselves in writing and establishing various avenues for responses are thoughtful approaches. Sending the question before the meeting allows individuals to contemplate their responses. For those hesitant to speak openly, alternative avenues such as emails or texts are encouraged, with a suggestion to maintain brevity—imposing a word count limit of, for instance, fifty words or less, or three to four sentences, ensures widespread participation.

Sixth, make sure you follow through with every aspect of discovery and implementation. The last thing you want to do is to go through this whole process and then skip the application phase. What this does in relationships, families, organizations, and businesses is it creates a cynicism that is hard to overcome. And what I've found in my time working with people is that they become less inclined to go through the process if they don't believe it's going to result in actual change. Sometimes people are shocked to find out that asking and getting the answers to hard questions was the easy part, but implementing the solutions was where they met all the real challenges.

Upon asking the questions and acquiring the answers, it becomes essential to methodically navigate through the responses and present them clearly. Whatever discoveries and lessons emerge, take actionable steps by devising explicit plans for implementation. Repeat this process consistently, refining and enhancing your approach with each iteration. You will attain mastery in this endeavor through repetitive practice.

CHAPTER 11

HARD QUESTIONS AND YOU

This final chapter addresses several aspects directly tied to the book's impact on individuals. Individuals must be cognizant of their predispositions, significantly influencing how they interpret and navigate hard questions. Recognizing others' predispositions is often simpler than acknowledging our own. Therefore, individuals require mirrors and trusted individuals who can offer loving yet candid insights.

A crucial step for all of us is how we are handling our past. Specifically, are we ensuring that our past is repositioned to work for us rather than against us? This process often demands effort, involving therapy or extended periods of reflection to reconcile and make sense of our past. Failure to heal from past experiences allows wounds to fester, subtly interfering when confronting challenging questions. Another consideration in your journey with hard questions is evaluating your current situation.

While writing this book, I currently find myself in a situation I never anticipated, and I acknowledge that some readers might be dealing with even more challenging circumstances. Concurrently, global events, such as conflicts in the Middle East and Europe, and various occurrences in America and worldwide, shape our current situations. It's essential to recognize that our surroundings affect us profoundly.

As permeable beings, we absorb a spectrum of stimuli—sounds, words, gestures, actions, social media, and perceived and genuine relationships. This awareness is crucial as we navigate the impact of our situations on the way we handle challenging questions. Additionally, consider your proficiency in handling relationships.

Remaining humble and acknowledging that not everyone shares an equal footing in engaging with hard questions is crucial. Individuals vary in readiness for growth and development, requiring time to enhance their effectiveness in dealing with challenging questions. Some may possess idiosyncrasies that impede the smooth process of asking and answering hard questions, necessitating personal growth in those areas. Encouraging self-grace and patience while simultaneously fostering honesty and self-motivation is essential. Emphasizing personal development and elevating one's relational skill level becomes imperative, facilitating more effective processing and benefitting from hard questions.

Understanding the internal dynamics within oneself involves gaining insight into thoughts, emotions, and personal contributions. This encompasses awareness and dedicated effort to assess the reasons and purposes behind these internal aspects. Achieving a regulated internal system is critical. A person with such regulation can benefit significantly from hard questions, unlike someone lacking this internal balance. For the latter, hard questions become challenging rather than advantageous. Additionally, taking ownership of one's narrative, rather than being dominated by it, is crucial to navigating hard questions. Narratives serve as the stories we construct to comprehend our existence.

Our narratives play a role in explaining and justifying our lives, beliefs, and behaviors. The recommendation is to ensure ownership of one's narrative, preventing it from exerting control. Lastly, maintaining proximity to core beliefs while embracing and challenging hard questions is advised, fostering a process of change with grace and peace.

EXERCISES

Individuals

Hard questions are the greatest tool for individuals. A "Hard question" is defined as a question that challenges a person's or entity's history, paradigms, beliefs, and behaviors and makes them uncomfortable. Read and answer the following questions to the best of your abilities. The best way to benefit from this exercise is to share it with someone.

What thoughts or emotions arise in you when you begin to interact with hard questions?

What are some solutions that could help you overcome the obstacles and objections you face as you attempt to answer hard questions?

What are some hard questions you should be asking yourself right now?

Do you think the way you are currently living is sustainable?

Who could help you to process through the hard questions you are asking yourself?

What are two things you could do to begin to benefit from hard questions?

CHAPTER 13

Leaders

Hard questions are the most powerful tools for leaders. "Hard questions" are defined as those challenging a person's or entity's history, paradigms, beliefs, and behaviors and makes them uncomfortable. Read and answer the following questions to the best of your abilities. The best way to benefit from this exercise is to share it with someone. Good luck!

What thoughts or emotions arise in you when you begin to interact with hard questions?

What are some solutions that could help you overcome the obstacles and objections you have towards hard questions?

As a leader, what hard questions should you be asking yourself right now?

Is your current way of leading sustainable?

Who could help you process the hard questions you are asking yourself?

What are two things you could do to begin to benefit from hard questions?

CHAPTER 14

Relationships

Hard questions are the most powerful tools for relationships. "Hard questions" are defined as those challenging a person's or entity's history, paradigms, beliefs, and behaviors and makes them uncomfortable. Read and answer the following questions to the best of your abilities. The best way to benefit from this exercise is to share it with someone. Good luck!

What thoughts or emotions do you experience when hard questions are asked of your relationship?

What are some solutions that could help you overcome the obstacles and objections you have toward hard questions?

What are some hard questions you should be asking about your relationships?

Is your current relationship sustainable?

Who could help you process the hard questions you are asking about your relationships?

What are two things you could do to begin to benefit from hard questions?

CHAPTER 15

Family

Hard questions are the most powerful tools for families. "Hard questions" are defined as those challenging a person's or entity's history, paradigms, beliefs, and behaviors and makes them uncomfortable. Read and answer the following questions to the best of your abilities. The best way to benefit from this exercise is to share it with someone. Good luck!

What thoughts or emotions do you experienced when hard questions are asked of your family?

What are some solutions that could help overcome the obstacles and objections you have toward having hard questions ask of your family?

What are some hard questions you should be asking about your family?

Is your current family dynamic sustainable?

Who could help you process the hard questions you are asking about your family?

What are two things you could do to begin to benefit from hard questions?

CHAPTER 16

Business

Hard questions are the most powerful tools for businesses. "Hard questions" are defined as those challenging a person's or entity's history, paradigms, beliefs, and behaviors and makes them uncomfortable. Read and answer the following questions to the best of your abilities. The best way to benefit from this exercise is to share it with someone. Good luck!

What thoughts or emotions do you experience when hard questions are asked of your business?

What are some solutions that could help overcome the obstacles and objections you have toward having hard questions asked of your business?

What are some hard questions you should be asking about your business?

Is your current business sustainable?

Who could help you process the hard questions you are asking about your business?

What are two things you could do to begin to benefit from hard questions?

CHAPTER 17

Organizations

Hard questions are the most powerful tools for organizations. "Hard questions" are defined as those challenging a person's or entity's history, paradigms, beliefs, and behaviors and makes them uncomfortable. Read and answer the following questions to the best of your abilities. The best way to benefit from this exercise is to share it with someone. Good luck!

What thoughts or emotions do you experience when hard questions are asked of your organizations?

What are some solutions that could help overcome the obstacles and objections you have towards having hard questions ask of your organizations?

What are some hard questions you should be asking about your organizations?

Is your current organization sustainable?

Who could help you process the hard questions you are asking about your organizations?

What are two things you could do to begin to benefit from hard questions?

CHAPTER 18

Cities

Hard questions are the most powerful tools for cities. "Hard questions" are defined as those challenging a person's or entity's history, paradigms, beliefs, and behaviors and makes them uncomfortable. Read and answer the following questions to the best of your abilities. The best way to benefit from this exercise is to share it with someone. Good luck!

What keeps us from asking hard questions about our city?

What could we do to create an environment where we could ask hard questions about our city?

What are some hard questions we should be asking about our city?

In your opinion, do you think your city is being ran in a sustainable way?

How could you help your city benefit from hard questions?

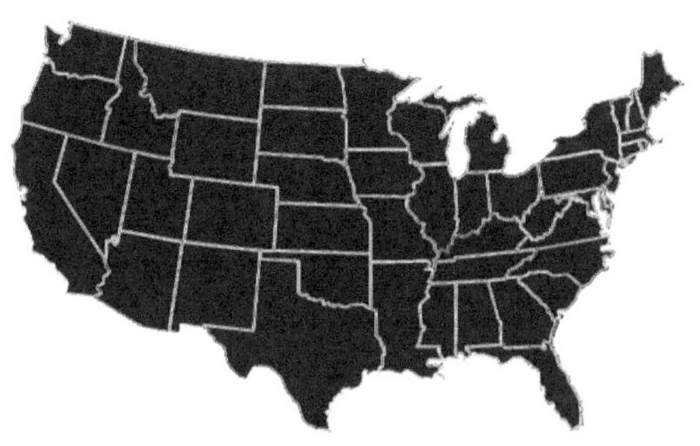

CHAPTER 19

States

Hard questions are the most powerful tools for states. "Hard questions" are defined as those challenging a person's or entity's history, paradigms, beliefs, and behaviors and makes them uncomfortable. Read and answer the following questions to the best of your abilities. The best way to benefit from this exercise is to share it with someone. Good luck!

What keeps us from asking hard questions about our state?

____
____
____
____
____

What could we do to create an environment where we could ask hard questions about our state?

____
____
____
____
____

What are some hard questions we should be asking about our state?

In your opinion, do you think our state is being ran in a sustainable way?

How could you help your state benefit from hard questions?

CHAPTER 20

Nations

Hard questions are the most powerful tools for nations. "Hard questions" are defined as those challenging a person's or entity's history, paradigms, beliefs, and behaviors and makes them uncomfortable. Read and answer the following questions to the best of your abilities. The best way to benefit from this exercise is to share it with someone. Good luck!

What keeps us from asking hard questions about our nation?

What could we do to create an environment where we could ask hard questions about our nation?

What are some hard questions we should be asking about our nation?

In your opinion, do you think our nation is being ran in a sustainable way?

How could we help our nation benefit from hard questions?

ACKNOWLEDGMENTS

I would like to thank all of the people who believed in me and gave me an opportunity to serve, lead, and consult in organizations, businesses and medical practices over the last thirty years. *Hard Questions* was birthed and raised in these environments.

I would also like to thank my closest friends for loving me enough to take the risk to ask me hard questions. By doing this, you have shown me their intrinsic worth and usefulness for my life. I would also like to thank them for putting up with all of the text messages and emails and half-baked thoughts, and hard questions that I have sent them over the years. Thank you for helping me to develop them! Thank you for never giving up on me and thank you for always encouraging me to be the serial intellectual.

I would like to thank Megan Jones and Tom Stolle, who worked with me to develop hard questions into an organizational exercise in 2023 and then encouraged me to write this book.

I would like to thank Dr. Lawrence Lenore for his presence in my life and for teaching me how to create an environment in my life, where hard questions can live and thrive are some of my best friends.

And I would also like to thank The Serial Intellectual Assistant, Lareine Concepcion. You are an amazing person with incredible gifts, and most of all a heart that is pure, kind, and beautiful. One of the greatest blessings God has ever given me is the opportunity to work with you. Thank you so much for helping me make this book of reality.

And last, I would like to thank God, who has never left me or forsaken me. I want to thank Him for all the hard questions he has sent my way. Whatever gifts, opportunities, and good I have, or am, or will be able to do, are all from Him and through Him and ultimately to Him.

ABOUT THE AUTHOR

Michael is a serial intellectual. He creates intellectual products that transform people and change the world. He was born in Los Angeles and lived there for almost four decades. In 2009, he moved to Baltimore City and has lived there for fourteen years. Michael has five beautiful adult children. Michael has a bachelor's degree in political studies with an emphasis in philosophy as well as a master's degree in divinity.

He is a certified Enneagram administrator, Scrum master and trained in project management. Michael has been coaching and consulting for twenty-five years. He has founded and led multiple nonprofit organizations. Michael is the author of six books; *100 Meditations: An Everyday Book for Everyday People; Don't Plant, Be Planted; Metamorphic Dictis; Be You; Social Revolution is Baltimore's Only Solution;* and *Hard Questions.* Michael is also the creator of the three personal development tools: Pause exercise, Emotional MRI, and Strategic Affirmations.

Michael is an accomplished triathlete and has completed all four distances. Michael's favorite sport is motocross, his favorite fast food is In-N-Out Burger, he is addicted to fresh Reese's Peanut Butter Cups, and absolutely love rottweilers. His favorite animals are killer whales and tigers. One of his favorite authors is Mark Twain, and one of his favorite quotes from him is "The two most important days of your life are the day you are born and the day you find out why."

9 798869 282071